Contents

Jay Ventress "What's That Sound"
Jay Ventress "Priorities"
Jay Ventress "Happy Face"
Danny O'Haco "Steel Girder"
Danny O'Haco "Who Framed Roger Rabbit"
Danny O'Haco "Stake Out"
Jeff Ohaco "Sell Out"
Danny O'Haco "Rodeo Cologne"
Joyce McNeal-Tolken "Jump from Limousine"
Spice Williams-Crosby "Roy 'Snuffy' Harrison"
Thomas Taylor Goodman "Ben Folds Five"
Danny O'Haco "The Rest of the Story"
Danny O'Haco "The Hang Up"

Introduction

I have been a member of the Screen Actors Guild for 34 years and worked on over a hundred productions as a stuntman and actor. Many friends in the business who inspired me to share our personal experiences, and those of the men and women who work behind the scenes.

You may recognize some movie titles or particular scenes mentioned in these pages. Many of these stories never made it into the final cut. Some are much more dramatic than what was in the final print.

My goal is to share these untold adventures for the first time in detail by the people who performed them. I wanted the reader to see what is involved in capturing a scene, how the performers prepare, and the mental mindset.

There is camaraderie among the stunt community. Practical jokes and light hearted humor run parallel to the uncertainty of the hazard or possible personal injury. Whether jumping off a sixty foot building or lighting one's self on fire all the stories presented here are real.

These personal experiences may fall from the editor's desk, but I am certain each are told in private, recanted to a friend, laughed about from time to time by those that were there.

My First Full Burn
By: Jay Torrez

I started hustling stunt coordinators when I was 23 years old, and living in Newport Beach, CA. I was very green at the time and didn't have much experience working in the business. At that point, the only thing that I had going for me was that I was a good athlete. I had just finished playing college baseball and was hoping to write the next chapter of my life. When coordinators asked if I did fire work I explained, "no, but I would be willing to learn." Truth be told, every time I thought about it, I cringed in my boots. I realize now, I felt this way because I had no idea how a stuntman could be fully engulfed in flames and survive.

As my career took off, I found myself working on big features where there was a real team element and everybody contributed to all tasks. I was working for a stunt coordinator who really took me under his wing. One day he asked me to help prep and safety one of the guys doing a full body burn. The guy doing the burn had all of the gear laid out on a table and he explained how everything was pieced together and carried out to his exact instructions.

He did 4 full burns that night and I was with him every step of the way. After that I picked the brains of many colleagues and mentors in order to learn more about fire. Eventually, I had a job offer from a coordinator to do several smaller 1/2 and 1/4 burns. I also had to prep/safety several other big burns, one of them involving a 40 foot high fall into boxes. This gave me a lot of confidence and the hope that one day I would get a chance to do my own full body burn. As time went on I finally got the call and here I am doing my first full burn at Santa Fe Studios for a "Stunt Lab" fire training seminar. In the photo, I am lit from head to toe with only fire gel on my face. It was one of the most memorable stunts that I have performed in my days as a professional stuntman!

It was a cold February morning in Santa Fe, New Mexico, but it was about to get really "hot" for me. I had worked many times with the stunt coordinator and the people who were helping with the burn so I felt very confident in our team. The stunt coordinator had us rehearse everything, from the order in which my protective clothing and wardrobe would be put on to the order in which putting out the fire would occur. He also had me rehearse my movement starting with the cue "he's lit" which started the classic Hollywood Stuntman Fire Dance. Then he had me lie down and the guys with the extinguishers would say, "He's out" to finish the rehearsal. We did this several times to ensure that everyone knew their job and we could carry out the stunt in a smooth fashion. Once everyone was comfortable with the timing and their task, it was time for the fun part.

We started with several layers of Carbon X protective layering (some of which were doused with freezing cold fire resistant gel) and finished with a set of denim jeans and a 100% cotton hoodie. One of my fellow stuntmen painted rubber cement all over my wardrobe to ignite the flames. He covered most of me except for my face, crotch and chest. We avoided those areas because I only had a hood on with no protection on my face. It would have been too close to my bare skin had we lit my chest, so we used that as my safety point and just covered my face in fireproof gel for extra protection.

When we were prepped and ready to go, the coordinator asked me if I was ready and I gave a nod and big thumbs up. He said, "Ok, light him up!" I took one final big breath and gave my guys the nod. With that, I was on fire and began my arm flailing, head bobbing dance with the flames. My whole back side was on fire from my ankles to the top of my head as well as my arms and legs. My stuntman fire dance, which was actually more like a fast walk that looked out of control, covered the distance of about 20 yards in a straight line and lasted only 15 seconds but those
15 seconds, became a very important part in my career.

To me it was a rite of passage into a small fraternity of stuntmen who have actually had the chance to do a full burn. As I got to the mark to be extinguished. I went down knees first, then hands and finally laid prone with my face down, arms and legs spread so that I didn't trap any flames between my limbs. I liked the sound of the fire extinguishers going "whew" and when they stopped I heard the stunt coordinator say "Jay, are you Ok?" I kept my mouth shut and held my breath, due to the fumes from the extinguishers. I gave a big thumbs up as they helped me up.

I very graciously smiled and gave nods to thank all of the people who were on set as I received a standing ovation. The stunt coordinator came up to me and asked me how I felt. I said "Awesome" with a big smile on my face. After I was stripped of my wardrobe and protective layers, I saw the footage recorded and I was very pleased with the way it went. The stunt coordinator told me, I did a good job and shook my hand. I was very gracious and thanked him for the opportunity. It truly was one of the most memorable gags I have performed as a professional stuntman!

Jay Torrez

Jay Torrez

Jay Torrez

Old School
By: Danny O'Haco

Our location was Davis-Monthan Air Force Base in Tucson Arizona. The movie, was "American Justice", starring Gerald McRaney and Jameson Parker. Second unit was filming a car chase and roll over sequence. We were in a bone yard of old retired World War II aircraft. It was the perfect backdrop.

We headed our bad guy off by slipping behind a B-52 bomber, and then we turned in the opposite direction. He tries to speed up and make the 90 degree turn but can't keep the wheels on the ground. The truck rolls over and comes to rest back on its wheels.

Billy Burton was directing second unit and also driving the roll over vehicle. In order to turn the truck over, a ramp was built. It was a wooden structure with boards wide enough for a tire to roll up. When the truck has two tires on the same side of the ramp, the driver will accelerate, crank the wheels at a 90 degree angle, the truck would roll over, and land back on its wheels again.

This was in the day when a stunt man would go to the seat and use a grab strap to hold himself down. It required great reflexes, and timing. Managing the speed and hitting the ramp at the perfect spot required skill. As the truck leaves the ramp the stuntman lays on the seat with his lap belt secure and grabs a strap, connected to the passenger seatbelt. Locking that arm down with his other arm and grasps it to his chest. This prevents any flailing of the arms and head. The roof could crush flat and the stunt man would remain safe. The glass was removed so there would be no danger of cuts or lacerations. The gas was drained out of the tank and a small bladder of gas would be the only gas in the vehicle. This helps prevent gas from splashing onto a hot wire or a spark and exploding into flames. The shot worked as designed and everyone was pleased. No injuries that day.

These days, the vehicle would have been retrofitted with a roll cage. The driver would be belted in with a four way harness, a helmet, and protective gear and padding.

Bill Burton is a stuntman who has bridged the old with the new, a rare breed in the film business. I'm glad I was on set that day to witness movie history. You couldn't find a man in this modern world of technology who would attempt a roll over using just a grab strap.

Up a Creek
By: Danny O'Haco

Bandits are expected to capture a stagecoach, have a gun fight and rob the passengers. Things don't always work out as scripted once the cameras are rolling. We were in Santa Fe, New Mexico filming "The Dangerous Trail" starring Sam Elliot. My role was to stop the stagecoach, tell the passengers," this is a hold up", promptly rob them and ride out of the scene. The director asked me to make my horse circle a few times before I mount up.

I circled my horse around a couple of times and swung my leg over the saddle. Suddenly the horse, busts in two, bogs his head and commences to bucking. I realize I am going over the other side and a tuck and roll is my only option, to survive this buck off. I launched out to the side expecting to hit the ground and roll onto my back. My right leg was still attached to the horse, I was slammed to the ground face first and snatched back into the air.

My spur rowel was entangled in the tasseled Mexican saddle blanket and my bucking horse was headed toward the dry creek bed.

I was drug down the creek bed, head and limbs bouncing along the rocks. I hadn't signed up for this gag. If my spur leather hadn't broken I might have left some body parts in that gulch.

Lucky is the word that described my condition, no broken bones, only a nice raspberry on my face.

Hanging by a Thread
By: Jeff Ohaco

"Lockup", was filmed at the Rahway State Prison, Rahway New Jersey. I was a stunt double for Sylvester Stallone. This facility was built in 1896, a maximum security prison. A scary place to visit. The worst of worst were doing time here.

There is a big dome structure in the center of the prison. In this scene Stallone's character plans to escape by jumping from the dome to the adjacent tower, if he makes it, he has a chance to escape. The height of the dome was approximately eighty feet.

The special effects crew seemed quite comfortable working at that height. A two foot catwalk had been constructed so we wouldn't slide to our deaths. I was shaking in my boots, trying to find any sense of calm. The stunt would involve me slipping on the wet surface of the Dome and sliding over the edge, but catch myself on the edge. I was to struggle to get back up and make my jump to the adjacent building. That's another story.

I was rigged with a harness, and to my alarm, a small quarter inch cable was attached. I wasn't sure that the cable would hold my weight, while dangling off the side of the Dome. The special effects man kept reassuring me the cable would hold me. He could see I was skeptical.

It was a freezing January morning, just before dawn. Cold temperatures made physical activities difficult. The Dome and catwalk were wet and slippery. Working at that height in those conditions made this stunt even more dangerous.

When the time came for "action", I said an act of contrition, and went over the edge. I clutched the lip of the roof and below me the camera was filming my distress. I hung there not wanting to put any weight on the cable, for fear it might snap. I held my breath waiting for the director to call cut. Finally I hear those words, "Cut and Print." I couldn't wait to get down. I didn't want to do that again.

The Jump
By: Jeff Ohaco

This is the second part of the story related to the Dome at Rahway State Prison. Earlier I had to dangle from the Dome and crawl back up, so I could jump to the adjacent tower and escape the prison yard. Doubling for Sylvester Stallone, just got a little dicey. I had to actually jump from the Dome to the next building.

We couldn't use the actual Dome like we did when I dangled from the edge. A mockup was built. It was on wheels so we could position it wherever we needed to. Sylvester is lifted to the top of the mock up Dome by a hydraulic lift, called a cherry picker. He surveys the jump, and thinks it should be a little further away from the adjacent building. He was actually considering doing the jump himself, but wasn't sure if a man could actually jump that far. The Dome was moved back a couple of feet so the distance to the tower was approximately fifteen feet. Without room to run, a flat footed jump would be the only way it could be done. I was to jump across and grab the ladder on the side of the tower and climb to the top.

Stallone asks, Frank Orsatti the stunt coordinator, "have Jeff give it a try". Frank was doubtful that it could be done from a standstill, and so was I. His advice was, try and sell it the best you can. I stood there on the catwalk trying to picture in my mind how I could do this. There was much excitement on the set that night. The crew members were taking bets on the outcome. Mostly against, which was not a morale booster for me.

The main camera was below me. That would be the best point of view to catch the leap across the chasm. The stunt crew set up crash pads and cardboard boxes to break my fall if I came up short. They were seventy percent sure that's where I would land.

When faced with challenges in my past I always did a ritual that would power me up. In my former career as a bronc rider I used this ritual more than once to make eight seconds. I would beat my chest rapid fire, stimulating the hypothalamus gland to release adrenaline.

I hear the Assistant Director yell "Rolling". I start beating my chest like there is no tomorrow! I hear "action" and I go in motion. I'm on auto pilot. I leave my secure place on the catwalk and fly through the air. My head slams into the ladder on the side of the tower. I have a split second before gravity takes over. As I fall toward the ground I manage to catch a rung with both hands. My momentum swings me back and slams me against the ladder face first. I scramble hand over hand to the top. My face felt warm and my vision blurred, blood was pouring down my face from a gash in my forehead. There was no pain, only a sense of complete exhilaration. The whole crew was clapping and cheering. What a day, I beat the odds!

Scuffle
By: Justin DeRosa

We were on location in Montana, filming "The Untouchables", staying at the Holiday Inn. I ran out of contact solution so I left my room which was on the second floor. I walked down stairs to the hotel lobby. I was half way down when I see Sean Connery talking to Art Linson, the Executive Producer. They were sitting on a couch. Off to the right of the lobby is a restaurant and bar.

I was almost down the stairs when two guys comeout of the bar and see Sean on the couch with Art. They approach Sean and said, quote: "So you're Bond, Mr. 007". These guys were "Three Sheets in the Wind" totally wasted. I thought they were going to ask for an autograph, but they started belittling him and getting in his face.

The situation quickly turned ugly as Sean got up from the couch and told them to back off. I saw that our producer was becoming alarmed. He said, quote: "This is my star, leave him alone"! Then fists started to fly. Sean was holding his own. Art saw me on the stairs and calls for me to jump in and break it up. I tackled the man nearest to me. We took out a table and lamp on the way down. Sean was on the floor wrestling with the second man. I have to say, Sean Connery can take care of himself. I threw no punches. Sean threw his share.

The police did come and they were hauled off to the slammer for assault. The next day on set Gary Hymes, our 2nd Unit Director and Stunt Coordinator, asked which one of us was involved in the fight with Sean Connery last night. I stepped forward and Gary said, "Art Linson wants to talk to you!"

Practical Joker
By: Tony Brubaker

It was 1980, we were on location in Phoenix, shooting the movie, "Used Cars", staring Kurt Russell and Jack Warden, directed by Robert Zemeckes. There was a group of stuntmen assigned to this motor home.

We were all hanging out in the motor home between shots, passing the time of day playing cards. This day wasn't going well for me, I lost what little money I had on me. I decided to have some fun with this crew. I went outside and started whooping and yelling, trying to disturb their concentration. I would put my shoulder under the wheel well and start shaking the motorhome. This went on for some time, pounding on the sides and going from window to window trying to create havoc. They were yelling and cussing me, I just laughed and kept on annoying them.

On one of the doors, there hung a curtain. I would grab and shake that curtain and howl. I was having a good time. I thought I was really agitating them. I went back around to the door with the curtain, and as I walk up to grab the curtain, it comes down and there standing is a guy with a bucket of water. I got it right in the face. I was practically drowning there in the desert. Everyone was laughing, I must have looked like a drowned rat at that moment. These men were practical jokers as well, and they got me good that day.

Through the Windshield
By: Steve Hart

"Tango and Cash", the movie was completed, but the producers didn't like the opening sequence. They wanted to reshoot the scene. I was hired by Jim Arnett to work stunts at the Palmdale set. I remember the first morning, Friday the 13th 1988. My then wife was pregnant with my daughter. I drove out to Palmdale at 5:00 am.

Frank Ferrara and I were sitting at the catering truck as a helicopter sets down. Jim Arnett stood next to our table and looked at me, at Frank, then back to me. He spit some Copenhagen and told me to, "Go put the clothes on". I went to get the clothes on, and then to hair and makeup. The hair girl was putting a bandana on my head and asked if I was going to need a pad underneath the bandana. I said I don't know what I'm doing. She laughed and said, "You'll soon find out". I was doubling for Robert Zdar the maniac cop.

I walked over to the set with Pat Romano the other stunt double. There was a Peterbuilt cab-over tractor sitting in the middle of the highway and the crew was setting up several cameras. The special effects crew was working on the Peterbuilt, and the normal controlled chaos that you find on a movie set was in full gear.

We walked up to the stunt coordinator who was standing in front of the tractor. He told us we were going to come through the windshield head first to the pavement. He stressed how important it was that we come through the windshield at exactly the same time. He asked, "Think you can do it?" We said, "Yes." Arnett spit some Copenhagen and said, "I've got five cameras on this and only want to do it once. "Don't screw it up!"

The special effects crew had put candy glass in for the windshield, and smoke effects on the wheels. The driver's seat was locked down, and the steering wheel was removed so we could squat on the seat. We climbed in very carefully not to touch the candy glass. Pat and I discussed timing, counting backwards from three to one, and go. We rehearsed the count down several times until we were comfortable with it.

 Sylvester Stallone came on set and was placed in front of the truck, we were ready to shoot the scene. The First Assistant Director yelled, "Rolling, Speed and Action". Pat counted aloud and we left at exactly the same time, but we came out in different body positions. It was the proverbial, "Fart Knocker." Eight feet to the pavement without any crash pads to land on. We only had knee, hip, and elbow pads on. When they called cut we got up to a bunch of applause from the cast and crew. I had a cut on the top of my head and it was bleeding, but otherwise I was in good shape. Pat didn't have a scratch on him.

We watched the video replay with Stallone and he was grinning from ear to ear. They took me to the hospital for a head and neck checkup as a precaution, and bandaged my cut. I was fine, and ready to go back to work. I worked in the helicopter chase sequences for three more days as the copilot playing a role, with dialogue.

When I saw the stunt in the theater it was amazing. The entire audience was in awe. It made me proud to be a stuntman. The stunt alone gave me a reputation in the business. Coordinators knew they could count on me when things got tough.

Steve Hart

Missed the
Mark By: R.L.
Tolbert

We were working out at Disney Ranch, shooting a
western, Sci-Fi show for television.   Buddy
Vanhorn was doing the stunt coordinating. He
picked me and Ross Loney, "Gander" to do a
saddle fall. This was a little different kind of saddle
fall, he wanted the saddle to come off with the
man. The saddles were rigged with a quick
release, to ensure this result. Depending on
where you wanted to land the buckle would be
placed on the opposite side of the saddle. Gander
had his own idea on how to set the quick release.
He puts the quick release on the right side which
was camera's side. I placed mine on the opposite
side. That way I would have some leverage to
push out of the saddle. When lining up a stunt,
you find a spot where you want to land and that
is your mark. During the shot set up, the camera
operator will pull focus to your mark. If you
miss the mark, the shot will be out of focus, and
you'll have to shoot another take.

We line up outside the shot and wait for the
Director to yell "Action". If the shot works as
planned and we execute properly, we would hear
the Director shout out "Cut and Print". On
"Action" we gallop in and hit our marks, trip the
quick release and fall into the shot, rider and
saddle together. I land on my spot, perfectly, but
Gander doesn't come off. He just continues on his

horse and rides past camera, and falls into a pile behind camera. He got a good laugh from the crew. When he tripped the release and tried to push off, he didn't have any leverage. He was just balancing on the horse's back, with no way of pushing away from the saddle. At that point he was just hoping gravity, would finish what he started. The Director wasn't happy with the outcome, and asked if we could try again. This time have Ross put the quick release on his left side, so he could land in the shot, with an exclamation point on, "In the Shot."

Hard Time

By: Steve Hart

In 1988 I was working for R.A. Rondell on the film "Hard Time on Planet Earth," I was doubling for Martin Kove. The script called for two police officers to chase our hero, Marty Kove, up a series of flights of stairs in an abandoned warehouse, eventually ending up on the roof with no way out. Our hero runs and jumps from one building to another landing on a giant tomahawk sign that gives way toward the street below. As luck would have it, there was a boat being pulled down the street by a pickup truck. The boat was an off shore fishing vessel with an open rear deck with two outboard motors. Our hero lands in the boat and gets away.

First Shot: A building to building jump. I jumped from one building about 40 feet (four stories) high to another building that was 30 feet high (three stories). The gap between the buildings was about 15 feet. Next I jumped from a parallel to the tomahawk and landed on the crosspiece below the tomahawk. I did that 3 time with a distance of about 6 feet, but was also 3 stories high with an airbag below for safety. Next as the tomahawk released and spit me out into space. I needed to stay upright as much as possible in order to get as much air time as possible. I did that stunt 5-6 times. We were done for the day.

On another day, we were downtown Los Angeles

around Bixel and Wilshire area. We have a 40 foot condor placed on an overpass above the street below. I had to stand on the outside of the condor while Eric Rondell drives the truck towing a boat down the street at what we agreed would be 7 mph. We did several rehearsals of me timing my jump without jumping. The boat contained a single layer of cardboard boxes and one stiffener placed on top with a canvas covering the boxes.

The jump was approximately 40 feet to the boat. I looked back, saw R.A. with his arms folded shaking his head. He wanted to have the truck speed up after I hit the boxes, so I had to do it one more time. I did, but my feet hit the motor on the back of the boat. Fortunately I didn't get hurt.

Durango
By: Walter Scott

Durango, Mexico was a great location for filming western movies, back in the day. I was doubling James Coburn in the Sam Peckinpah film, "Pat Garrett and Billy the Kid."

It was December and Christmas was just a few days away, Sam was not letting any of the crew go home to Los Angeles for the holiday, for fear that they wouldn't return to Mexico to finish the film.

At the same time, John Wayne was filming in Durango. I had friends working on that show. John had a private jet that he would use to fly back and forth to Los Angeles. He would let some of his crew go when they could get away. This Christmas he would be flying in to LA and then right back to Durango. There was an open seat, and my friend said he could hold it for me if I wanted to go home for Christmas. I gladly accepted, but needed to do it in secrecy. We had strict orders not to leave Mexico. We would be shut down anyway, and nobody would miss me.

Upon my return to Durango on the Duke's jet, I was told Mr. Peckinpah was aware I had gone to Los Angeles. Expecting to be fired or reprimanded, I waited for the word. No word came, instead I was told to report to the set. Each day I showed up and dressed in full wardrobe, a skull cap, and full beard. Day after day I waited to double for James Coburn. This went on for a long time. I sat in the heat sweating profusely for hours every day. It finally dawns on me that James Coburn hasn't been on the call sheet for weeks.

Rodeo Girl
By: R.L. Tolbert

We were shooting a movie for cable TV called Rodeo Girl. Katherine Ross was playing the lead, the story about a Rodeo Champions life. We hired a stunt double for Katherine. She would do the bronc riding. The director and I talked about what he needed to make the shot work. At this point we hadn't shot a really good bucking scene. He wanted more from our stunt double. According to the stunt double, the horses weren't good enough. She needed a better bucking horse. When it came time to shoot the bucking horse scene, they asked me to pick one I thought would surely buck. I had just the one for her.

The horse came from the Flying U bucking string. Resistol, a big black stallion, bucked mostly as a saddle bronc, but could go either way. Sometimes he was bucked in the bareback riding, just for a change. Bareback riders didn't like him. He was a bucker, and I had heard our stunt- double say, she needed a better bucking horse. I knew he wouldn't let us down.

We loaded the chute with this twelve hundred pound bronc. She climbs down and gets her seat, with two hands down. Nods to the gate man, the gate cracks open, he bales out, and kicks straight over his head.

She didn't even start him, got drilled face first, like a yard dart in the arena. Didn't even clear the chute gate. For the rest of the show, I never heard a word about the horses not bucking hard enough.

The Unintentional

Stunt By: R. L. Tolbert

The movie is titled "Far and Away," staring Nicole Kidman, and Tom Cruise. The location for filming is in Billings Montana, the scene is a re-creation of the Oklahoma Land Rush. There are people on foot, horseback, wagons, bicycles, any means of transportation. I was hired as a stunt man rigger because I have a lot of experience with wagons and teams. My job was to prep wagons for the stunt shots. The wagon beds were interchangeable in case one was damaged during a stunt. Just take it back to the shop and replace the old damaged bed with a new one and be ready for the next shot.

A cable is attached to the rear axle, the other end to a cement anchor point. When the wagon reaches the length of the cable, the wagon will be torn in two. This was our intention for the first shot. The rear axle comes off and the occupants are flung out when it crashes, but the wagon bed does not come apart as it is supposed to. Apparently, the effects team forgot to score the boards on the wagon bed. We take the wagon back to the shop, and the boards are scored so the wagon bed will come apart.

The wagon is again hooked to a cable, and loaded with nine stunt men. Their job is to fly off the wagon, do a tuck and roll, get up and chase down someone on horseback, jump on and ride off. The scene works out like this. The wagon hits the end of the cable, the axel comes off, the wagon breaks in two, and the stunt men are flung out and hit the ground. A runaway wagon wheel has come off during the wreck and is headed straight for the stunt man, Chris Brannon. He never sees it coming. It rolls right over his chest. It must have weighed a couple hundred pounds. Chris jumps up and takes off running, as if nothing had happened, catches up to a horse and rider, vaults on like a pony express rider, and continues with the scene. If you were watching the movie, you would have thought, "wow," what good timing.

The Catapult
By: Danny O'Haco

The movie, "Rambo III" starring Sylvester Stallone and Richard Crenna, was filming just west of Yuma in the desert. The location was to resemble Afghanistan. The stuntmen, dressed as Afghanistan rebels, defend Rambo against the Russians. Rebels are all mounted, and will be charging the Russian troops. In this shot, 20 or so horseback rebels were in our group. To our left flank is another group of mounted rebels.

On action we attack the Russian forces from both sides. Our horses were not familiar with gunfire, explosions, or fire. It was hard keeping the horses from running off. Most of the stunt men were excellent riders. There were some extras who claimed they could ride but were not doing well in this situation. Every man was for himself.

We line up with our horses and automatic weapons, awaiting action. This would be the Master Shot, then the director would cover the action with actors and shoot the close ups. The scene was of a grand scale with all the rebels coming from two sides and the Russian army in the middle. Multiple cameras were running.

The explosions are set off and we are shooting from our horses as we race across the desert to engage the enemy. Some stuntmen were instructed to take a saddle fall while others raced forward.

My group was to move forward while the group from the left would merge with our group and attack head on. I could see some stunt men taking their falls, while their horses raced forward out of control. There was going to be a collision of horses if someone didn't stop or change direction. I tried to rein my horse out of the group hoping I would miss a t- bone collision. It was no use, my horse had taken his head and was determined to run straight ahead full blast.

One loose horse was on course for our group, and I could see someone was going to get hit broad side. These kinds of collisions can be very dangerous for horse and rider. There were two or three horses to my left, a few in front of me. I thought surely one or more of them would be taken out.

This runaway horse threads his way through our group missing everyone except me. I had a second to decide how to take the collision, I kicked both stirrups loose and tilted forward. We collided almost broad side, my horse's head about mid-saddle. Both animals are going down, I am launched into the air over the front end of both horses. I have an AK-47 in my arms with a shoulder strap. My instinct was to tuck and roll, not knowing if I would be trampled by the horses behind me.

The sand was a blessing, and my tuck and roll was perfect. I roll up on my knees with the machine gun blazing. I didn't hear, "Cut" so I just keep playing soldier. Now I'm out of ammo and realize that I am in the center of the scene. I take a hit from enemy fire and go down.

Next day when viewing, "dailies" the scene is shown. It was a good scene of some impromptu acting on my part, but it never made it into the movie.

Richard Crenna and Danny O'Haco. Rambo III
Photo By: Dave Friedman

Double Hock
By: Samie Brakenbury

We were filming "Comes a Horseman" staring James Cann, Jane Fonda, and Richard Farnsworth. I doubled for Jane, and we did a lot of roping. H.P. Evetts doubled James and our stunt coordinator Walter Scott wanted to motivate us. He knew how good a roper H.P. was, but he wasn't sure about me. He said I will give you a $100.00 bump for every catch. We had to chase these steers through the brush at full speed, rope them and drag them past camera. We did the scene six times that day and we caught six steers.

One the way back to the Hotel we are all in the van, Walter speaks out and says, "oh by the way I can only pay $50.00 a catch". I guess he didn't figure we would catch every time. He said the reason was a budget issue. I had to laugh, he didn't think this cowgirl could throw a loop with such accuracy. He didn't know I grew up on my father's ranch and we roped all the time.

Working with Richard Farnsworth was wonderful, he was a very kind and generous man. He actually went to rodeos with my father when they were young. Sure do miss my friend Dick.

Hit the Skids

By: Danny O'Haco

I was working on a television movie called "Blood Vows" the story of a mafia wife. The scene we were going to shoot, would involve a helicopter, and three stunt men. The target would be the wife of the Mafia mobster.

Our plan was to fly into the compound, land by the pool and nab the wife. We got together with the stunt coordinator, and worked out what each man was to do on landing. I was supposed to step out on to the helicopter skid, as we set down and hit the ground running. I have my automatic rifle slung over my shoulder so it sits in front of me waist high. Seems everything is working according to the plan. We descend slowly to the landing spot. I start to work my way to the edge of the seat, getting ready to make my move.

There is no way to communicate with the pilot from the back seat. The noise is deafening there is no sense yelling. If you had visual contact you could use hand signals, but that wasn't going to work in this situation.

We were just inches off the landing spot, so I step out on the skid. As I do, suddenly the pilot starts to ascend rapidly. He had received a radio contact from the director to abort, and re approach. I am out on the skid, with nothing tethering me to the chopper. When you are in flight the skids are much lower than they would be after landing. They work like a shock absorber, making the landing smoother. I froze clutching the side of the seat at the floor board, as we rise to 300 feet or so. I had heard about people freezing when panicked, especially from heights. There was a stunt man across from me in the other seat. He just looked at me like, "what the heck are you doing"? He didn't tap the pilot on the shoulder to let him know that I was in a dangerous situation. I had to get out of this myself. I started to make myself breathe and calm my heart rate. Once I had calmed down some I started to raise my leg up to the step that I had used when boarding. It wasn't where I thought it would be. Without that step there is no way to hoist my body into the chopper.

When the helicopter is on the ground, the step is just a foot up from the skid, when in the air it is another six to eight inches higher. I am deathly afraid to look for it, fearing my grip on the seat might slip. The chopper just continues to ascend into the sky. The people on the ground looked like ants.

I desperately keep trying to find that step with my boot. Carefully moving it across the fuselage like a blind man with a cane. I did finally locate it, a sigh of relief came over me. I was going to get back inside. I put my boot on that step and made a monster push and landed inside.

Since I experienced this firsthand I will never second guess a person who is panicked. It's all different when it's happening to you.

First High Fall
By: Thomas Taylor Goodman

This was Danny O'Haco's first high fall. We were filming Three Amigos in Tucson. The scene was for El Guapo to ask Paco the guard on the roof, to raise his hat so he could shoot it with the new gun he was buying. The fall required Danny (Paco) to engage with El Guapo, get shot and fall off the roof. The air bag was off to the back of the building. This was a blind fall, not being able to see the bag before leaving the roof.

Danny crawled up on the roof and stood at the corner of the building, looking things over and deciding how to hit the bag. This air bag was not designed for a fall of that height. The building was two stories tall. This was the first time the air bag had been used on this shoot. Spotters were placed around the edges to safety Danny if he should over or under shoot the bag.

What had been over looked in the setup were the vents on the sides of the air bag which needed to be open so it would collapse when impacted.

Danny made his fall on cue, his body twisting trying to find a sweet spot on the air bag. That's when things went wrong. Since the vents were closed the airbag works like a trampoline. I was on the corner when Danny hit the bag and bounced. As Danny is flying off the bag my reflexes took over and I grabbed him by the collar. It's a good thing I was there, you see there was a canyon full of Arizona cactus just waiting for our stuntman. Danny ended up doing the fall 4 times, good job Paco.

Toyota
By: Danny O'Haco

We were shooting a Toyota truck commercial in the desert north of Scottsdale. The shot was two trucks driving side by side down the road. From out of the brush, comes a gang of outlaws. They ride along the side of the lead truck and an outlaw jumps from his horse to the bed of the truck. Their slogan for Toyota was, "Get that Toyota Feeling". The man jumping to the truck was supposed to spread his arms and legs out to express that feeling.

I was hired to drive one of the trucks. They wanted two trucks in the shot at the same time with the outlaws coming up from behind. We lined up and shot the first take. From the camera angle there was not enough time in the air to express that "Toyota Feeling".

We lined up again and shot take two, three, four and maybe five. The stunt rider was wearing out, and the director didn't like what he was seeing. I went over to the director and told him I could do the jump. We talked some more and the decision was made. I was going to do the next take. I set my step on the side of the saddle as high as I could so when I pushed off from the step I would get some height to spread my arms and legs. We shoot the scene and I don't get any more height than the other stuntman. Now the pressure is on, could I deliver like I claimed I could?

Joe Brown was one of the outlaws and he rides over and suggests that I get on and ride double with him. I would crouch down behind him as he races up to the truck. Once alongside the truck, I would spring off the back of his horse and get the height that was needed. This would be tricky because I would have to balance on the butt of the horse.

I needed to stay behind Joe, down low, so I couldn't be seen. His horse was a good sized one, and it wasn't that tough to balance myself in the crouch. We are moving at a pretty good clip. My timing needs to be perfect to spend enough time in the air and still land in the back of the truck. There is only one spot where this will work and I need to find that spot. I push off and shoot into the air, doing the spread eagle the way they wanted. I got that "Toyota Feeling" on film, thanks to my friend Joe Brown.

Eagle Butte
By: Blain Nordvold

The film "Born to Buck" with Casey Tibbs was filmed in Fort Pierre, South Dakota. Some four hundred wild mustangs were gathered for the movie. After filming ended Casey left the herd of mares and a couple of stud horses at our place, outside of Ft. Pierre. After a couple of years, Casey called and wanted us to gather up the mares, he wanted to sell some of the younger ones.

At his request my brother Jud and I trailed the herd to Eagle Butte where we could sort and load out the younger horses. We corralled the herd, and waited for Casey to show. He shows up in his big Cadillac with another guy, and they had been drinking some.

He steps out of the car with a jug of Jack Daniels in one hand, and climbs into the corral to survey the herd. He starts after one of the stud horses, corners him and grabs the tail. This stud horse is dragging Casey all over the arena. And he is whooping and hollering "Let er Buck you wild sons a bitches." I don't know why that stud never kicked him dead center with both feet, he sure had the opportunity.

Casey paid us off and we had a few drinks together, laughed and reminisced about the old days. The next day Jud and I trailed that herd right up Main Street, on our way back home. This caused some folks to be very unhappy with us. Eagle Butte hadn't seen that much excitement in some time, and probably hasn't since.

Oscar
By: Bud Graves

I was just thinking about my friend Ben Johnson, 1952 World Champion Team Roper, a great actor as well. Wag Blessing was my uncle, 1947 World Champion Bull Rider who got me a job cleaning Ben's corals. It was a hot summer day and I had finished up my chores, sweat was running down my face. I banged on the screen door and said to Ben I was done cleaning. He could see I was hot and asked if I wanted to come into the kitchen and get a soda.

He asked if I was hungry, and I said yes, so he made me a peanut butter sandwich. He asked me how I was doing in the junior rodeo. I said I was leading the bull riding, and that brought a big smile to his face. He said son I'm proud of you and he pulled out a 50 dollar bill and handed it to me. I was shocked, and very pleased. I asked if I could see his trophy collection. We walked into the living room and there were all these beautiful trophies from Madison Square Garden, and cities from all over this country. In the middle of all these rodeo trophies was a statue of Oscar. He had won the Oscar for the part he played in "The Last Picture Show."

He asked what trophy did I like the best out of all these, I could not make up my Mind. He asked, what about Oscar? I really didn't know what the Oscar was so I picked it up and looked it over.

Out of all, I said, this is my least favorite. He started laughing, I didn't understand why he got a kick out of what I said. He gives me a big hug and says you're a beautiful boy. I didn't know what he meant until years later. He was a marvelous man and he was my friend. I called him once a month for years until he died. I miss my very good friend Ben Johnson.

The Salt River Crossing
By: Danny O'Haco

I was hired to wrangle horses on the production of a commercial for Wrangler Jeans. The principle characters were World Champ Gary Leffew, John Quintana, and the lovely Mary Catherine Brannaman.

The scene called for driving a herd of horses across the Salt River, and filming the splash and the beauty of the desert in the background. It was a crisp February morning, and I had layers of clothes on, vest, goose down jacket, gloves, long johns, cowboy boots and spurs.

We thought we found a shallow crossing that the horses could traverse without having to swim. The river was running fairly wide at this point, and the current was moving fast. To my left was a bend in the river where the water turned into a giant eddy. We had heard that some kids who were out tubing last summer had drowned there. They were caught in the eddy and couldn't fight the current. It pulled them under.

Our herd of about 50 head, entered the river. Strung out in a long line, I could see the lead horses swimming for the opposite shore. The little horse I was on was doing fine until he stepped off into the main channel. That's when he started to flounder about, his whole body turned to one side, and the current was pushing him sideways. I saw my weight was causing problems so, I just pushed off thinking he would right himself. We split at that point and he moved forward seeming to have recovered. I am now in the middle of the current treading water. From the camera's point of view, up on the cliff, the only thing visible, was my hat.

I realize my situation and look for the shore line. It can't be more than 20 yards away. I should be able to make it. However, my soaked clothing began sinking me like an anchor weight on my shoulders. I keep swimming straight across, but the current is pulling me down toward the bend, and the giant eddy. I am now getting winded and realize I haven't gotten any closer to the shore line. Another wrangler is running down the bank trying to figure out how he can pull me to shore. The current is moving me down river fast, and I am exhausted. It dawns on me that there is a chance I could drown in this river. It is looking worse by the minute.

The wrangler has run down stream and entered the water waist deep, he was going to grab me as I struggled by. His plan worked. He grabs me by the jacket and hauls me in. I collapsed, gasping for air.

Looking back I probably could have touched bottom and walked out, it was that shallow close to shore, but that never occurred to me. The mind has a survival mode, and swimming to that shore was my goal. Thank God my fellow wrangler had enough sense to move down stream and catch me going by. The funny thing about all this is my hat never got wet.

False Bottom
By: R.J. Chambers

In the early 90's I was a stunt coordinator on a CBS TV series entitled "Ned Blessing." Actor Brad Johnson, a very good cowboy in his own right, played Ned Blessing. The setup for the first shot of the very first day of shooting was discussed and the following is what we wanted to shoot: Ned was to be on the run on horseback, fleeing from Banditos that clearly outnumbered him. I was to double Ned and as I came to a river I was to cross it on horseback in a hurry.

We wanted the water to be approximately 2 feet deep, so when the horse I was riding crossed at a pretty good lick, there would be a lot of splashing and action. After I reached the far side of the river, I was to quickly dismount and unsheathe my rifle. I was then to get in position to open fire on the Banditos and there would be a cut.

At this point, Brad was to take my place and begin plucking off Banditos as they splashed into the river pursuing his character "Ned Blessing." Brad being a good cowboy and a great hand with a rifle gave us the luxury of whatever kind of overlap we might need once I got across the river and reached the bank.

We had scouted the locations for the river crossing during the previous week. Others and I waded into the river a couple of times and it looked great. The river bottom seemed as hard as the road and the water depth was just right for what we wanted to do. On the morning of the shoot the crew was getting everything ready. I and the Banditos stuntmen and the wranglers started to cross the river with the horses that we were going to use in the opening shot. Everything looked good until we got out into the middle half of the river and the horses started to break through the river bottom. The river bottom had a very hard crust but the weight of a horse and rider was causing the horses to fall through the bottom much like they would have done if they had been walking on hard crusted snow. Every time a horse would try to pull itself out and onto the hard crust he would break through it again and be in the same bad situation. We eventually got the horses out of the river and on hard ground.

After a discussion we decided to change our location on the river to a spot where the water was deep enough that when I jumped his horse into the river I would not touch bottom and have to swim across. We also decided that if there was a little more space between me and the pursuing Banditos, they could be plucked off as they neared the jumping off spot on the river bank. This would allow some of the Banditos to be shot off their horses and into the water and some to retreat. This would also give us the action of loose horses along the bank.

We hauled the horses to the other side of the river, figured out what our frame was and got ready to shoot the scene. The horse I had intended to ride was too stressed from trying to cross the river earlier, so we picked another horse I was familiar with, who was a good match for the "hero" horse. I looked the jumping off spot over, but I never took my mount up to the river bank to look things over. I figured the less he knew about what was up there, the more likely the two of us would make a successful jump.

The spot we had chosen had about a four or five foot drop to the water. It all sounds pretty simple, but there were some pitfalls. I had a high backed saddle with a bedroll tied to it. Also, high boots that could soon fill with water, big spurs, and a leather jacket with lots of fringe. I was wearing a big hat, a lariat was tied to the saddle, and they needed me to be holding a lever action Winchester incased in a beaded Indian scabbard. The goal was for me to have all the gear intact when I reached the other side. Now, if that isn't enough, I can't swim. I know if the old bay props or scotches when we get to the bank of the river, his momentum will take him over the edge and we will more than likely go end over end into the river.

We pick the start mark and the time to jump and swim. Action is called and I ride the bay hard to the river bank. As we get right to the bank I feel him for a fraction of a second, but he didn't prop. Luckily, he had used the squat to help him jump from the bank out into the river. When we came up I was still right in the middle of him with all my props and trappings. We swam to the other side, I dismounted, we cut and the actor took over.

Later in the day the Texas fellow that owned the horse I made the jump with, told me he had been in a situation at a ranch where they jumped some horses into a river to swim across and one of the cowboys had come off his horse. A swimming horse struck him in the head and the cowboy drowned.

"Ned Blessing" was a great TV series to work on. To this day, I wish CBS had not pulled the plug on it.

Gana La Verde
By: Bill Brown

I always in the back of my mind, wondered, when we die, will we know when the time has come, and this is it?

The year is 2005 in Los Angeles, California. I was working on a Mexican version of our American "Fear Factor" TV show, "Gana La Verde."

Our stunt this day was with a tanker half full of water where our contestants would gather 3 flags from inside. The fastest time wins. Well, I always tried to do the stunt first to make sure everyone would be safe.

The only way in to the tanker was past a hole in the middle, so I built a span set (rope ladder), to go in, then climb out. My camera man was harnessed in on one end of the tanker with a underwater camera. My idea was that on action, have the driver of the tanker pop the clutch to make waves in the water inside the tanker.

Before action, I was standing in waist deep water. When the tanker started, suddenly all the water was at the other end, then it was coming my way, all at once. It took me out and I was in an upside down water trap. My camera man was ok. He was in a swing harness. The man on the outside port hole was harnessed to the truck. He couldn't really see inside. They were ok, but I had not thought about safety-ing myself. I had gone four times back and forth, going around upside down and running out of air. I remember coming to the end where my camera man was, and trying to grab him to stop myself, but the water was too violent. I couldn't get out. I remember thinking "This is it". Just for a second, I was ok with that, then all of a sudden I thought, "Hell no! It's no ok!"

I opened my eyes and saw my span set ladder. I remember aiming my head through the middle and wrapping my arms around the side, pulling myself up and screaming "Cut!" "Cut!" The man on the top had radioed to the truck driver to stop. The camera man got unbelievable footage of me going around and around, like the devil had ahold of me. It seemed like the most powerful force I have ever felt. Grabbing the ladder to stop me from the whirl of water ripped my wetsuit at the shoulder, but I was unhurt.

We did the show, but the truck only went five miles an hour, and we didn't hardly even get the contestants wet.

Getting Even
By: R.L. Tolbert

Sometimes what comes around goes around. Back in my early days I rode bulls. I was at the Scottsdale Rodeo one year, and drew this fighting bull. He was cow horned and couldn't really hook you, but he could sure camp all over you. I get off the bull, and immediately he is on me, snorting in my pockets. I'm moving as fast as I can, looking for some help. I needed a clown bullfighter to distract him. I get to the fence and look over at the clowns, Chuck Hensen and Larry McKinney. They were having a good laugh at my expense. I knew these guys forever, and they were practical jokers. They just wanted to see my face, when I got to the fence.

A few years later Chuck and I are working on the movie "The Three Amigos". I was doing stunts and Chuck was wrangling horses. Wouldn't you know it, he was assigned to my horse. Juan, my big thoroughbred was a handful to ride. I could handle him, but anybody else who tried, found themselves wanting to get off.

We shot a chase scene with horses running down the road. The horses were all excited, Juan is dancing around, I am having a hard time keeping him lined out. When the Director called for lunch we all headed back to the feed truck. Old Juan knew that it was time to eat and he would make a bee line for the hay wagon.

Chuck comes up and says, "I'll take him back for you." He starts to lead him off.   I suggested he ride Juan back, seeing how far away we were. I knew what Juan would do, and I remembered how those clowns laughed at my expense, while that bull in Scottsdale mopped the floor with me.

Chuck mounts Juan, and away they go. First, Juan rears, and then starts caprioling, dancing toward the trucks. Chuck is having a hard time controlling him, and they are headed toward the Director and the camera crew. They meet on the bridge. The Director and camera crew are forced to bail over the side, or get run down.

They were not happy about that, you could hear them cussing Chuck up one side and down the other. I had to laugh, thinking to myself, "paybacks are a bitch."

The Back Over
Danny O'Haco

In the movie "The Three Amigos" I was a stunt double for Tony Plana, who played the part of Jefe. If you remember the movie, Jefe is shot in the end, but assures El Guapo that he is still here (alive), and then falls on his face dead from being shot.

The part you didn't see was the first take, a "back over" off a rearing horse. I had never reared this horse and the wrangler told me, you really need to take his head, if you want a good rear.

This isn't my first rodeo and I wasn't going to let this horse make me look bad. If the stunt went as planned, as the horse reaches his zenith, I would roll off his back to the ground on my feet, doing a back summer salt.

On cue, I lifted on the reins and added a little spurs. Up we came, adrenalin pumping. The horse kept coming higher and higher, while I rolled off the back. Too late to abort, the wreck was about to happen.

He reared alright, goes all the way over backwards. We both hit the ground in a heap. I thought surely he would crush my chest. I got up, dusted myself off, not a scratch on either of us. "Take two," is in the movie.

Danny O'Haco and Kathleen O'Haco "Three Amigos"

Stair fall
By: Thomas Taylor Goodman

I was working on the film,"TripFall" with John Ritter and Eric Roberts, on the Santa Monica Pier. The scene required Eric the bad guy, to kidnap John our hero. The pier was crowded with tourists so in order to get the shot things had to change. I was asked to go get dressed as a homeless beach bum. I padded up with elbow pads, knee pads and a back pad to minimize bruising. There was no way to pad my head. My clothing concealed the padding.

John was to run to the stairs, pay no attention to the homeless man. Eric was to push me into the rail and get down the stairs as fast as possible. The camera was set up at the bottom of the stairs in the sand. The stairs were from the top of the pier to the beach some thirty steps below.

On action I was on the stairs waiting for the actors to pass by. John passes first, and being a professional looked scared. Eric then passes and bumps me, I start to tumble, head over heels, as I approached the last 4 steps I saw Eric had cleared a path for me to roll past camera. As I cleared the camera operator I jumped up and asked if I should do it again.

John's eyes were wide open and he grabs me and gives me a bear hug, and says we got the shot. He says, Tom you stuntmen scare me to death. The coolest thing was I got to have dinner with John and his wife that night.

Danny O'Haco "Three Amigos"

When Your Numbers Not Up
Eddie Braun

The morning started out really nice, pretty much a typical day. We were shooting a commercial for Chevrolet, and we would be shooting Ariel shots from our helicopter. Our director had a huge fear of flying, and asked me to handle everything from the air with the drivers below. No sweat, I got this.

We wanted to go for another take, so we go back to one and we are set. Over the head set you hear a loud bang, then the pilot "oh shit." In that instance I knew my life would change dramatically. Those seconds seemed like an eternity as the ground rushes up from below. The cars that looked like dots just a second ago now are now coming into focus.

You wonder if it's going to hurt much, there's a sense of peace as you are convinced you are about to meet your maker. No screams, no terror, just time for a deep breath, a short prayer and brace for impact.

With eyes closed you feel like you're being tumbled in a washing machine and hit by a loud freight train. Seems like forever, when is it going to end. Still no pain at this point this isn't so bad. Then all quiet, calm for a moment. My next recollection is I slowly opened my eyes, not sure of what I'm about to see. I heard moaning, no sign of blood, I'm in one piece not a scratch. Now things start to move in fast forward, I can smell smoke, I hear a commanding voice of none other than Conrad Palmisano standing next to me, he grabs me with what seemed like superhuman strength, assuring me that he would get me out of the burning wreckage. The pilot and camera man were rushed to the trauma center. Me I am not going anywhere.

It took a moment to gather my thoughts, grab a cool bottle of water. All around me people were hustling back and forth. The Director was sick to his stomach, I could hear the First Assistant Director, asking if we could salvage any film from the helicopter camera.

This changes the schedule, move to another location, lunch break, still plenty more to film today.

Things back to normal, meal penalties, and magic hour, overtime, and turnaround issues. No this would not be my last day on this earth, but fade into just another day at the office.

Once Upon a Time, Many Moons Ago.
By: Eddie Matthews

I have worked on over 200 movies, many of those mega budget productions with huge stunts, doubling stars such as Robert DeNiro, Sly Stallone, Mark Walberg, Anthony Hopkins, and many others. Some of my fondest memories have been working on smaller more intimate sets, many of those family films that actually have the potential to entertain, but also touch the hearts and minds of kids, families and sometime the actors working in the movie.

One of these movies I had the opportunity to stunt coordinate was a faith based family film produced by Billy Graham's film organization World Wide Films. The movie was called "A Vow to Cherish" about a man's wife who was showing signs of Alzheimer's, and she was becoming more and more out of touch with reality.

The Husband of this women was becoming involved with another women, a beautiful lady that he was associated with. He was faced with the dilemma that many will face in life, to remain faithful, when these temptations are presented. The character in this movie ultimately chose to honor his marriage, but not without much struggle. He chose to stay faithful to his wife to the end.

The star of this movie was Ken Howard, a Tony and Emmy award winning actor known for "Crossing Jordan" and as Coach in the TV series "White Shadow." Currently he is the president of the Screen Actors Guild.

A couple of things that make this movie memorable to me was my 4 year old daughter, Abi, got her SAG card playing my daughter in the movie. My 7 year old son Aaron also worked on the film as stunt kid.

My daughter, worked in a stunt scene where she was pushing her baby buggy in our driveway near the street where the stunt was going to take place. Renowned stunt women Jeannie Epper, (doubling the wife with Alzheimer's) drove the car down the street, out of control hitting mailboxes, driving over the sidewalk and through front yards. She swerved into my driveway where my daughter was pushing her baby buggy. She hits the buggy, and narrowly misses my daughter as I pull her out of harm's way just in the nick of time.

My memory of this film is not just how it impacted the audience, but also how it affected the people that worked this movie. Shortly after the filming of this movie Ken Howard was diagnosed with kidney failure. He was going to die if he didn't get a kidney transplant. Jeannie Epper the stunt women on the show, a real life hero and a true Christian, stepped forward away from her stunt career and into real life to donate a kidney to Ken, saving his life while possibly sacrificing her future career.

In this day and age where ego, selfishness and self- promotion are the norm, sacrificial giving such as this is rare. It's heartwarming when I see Ken on a talk show or in an interview thanking Jeannie for her selfless act that saved his life.

This reminds me that God has a plan, his purpose and timing are in his hands, if we just trust him. We as stunt people need his wisdom and blessing every time we walk through those doors, to keep us safe from harm and injury. His intervention in our lives will provide for us the right person, when in need. We hope that if someone needs us we will be there.

Anthony Hopkins and Eddie Matthews

In Harms Way
By: Ryan Happy

My brother Sean and I were working on the "The Lone Ranger" starring Johnny Depp. While shooting the train sequences we did a lot of stunt work. We were doing transfers from our horses to the train and from the train to our horses. Richard Bucher and Jordan Warrack were standing in their saddles at a full run and leaping to the train. Now that is difficult.

In this scene, Sean was pulled off the train by a Ranger, his bullwhip wrapping around Sean's ankle. Once Sean is jerked off the train, he is to roll on his side, beside the train as it's moving down the track. If you have ever tried to roll in a straight line you know it's very difficult.

Sean started to veer toward the train, he was unaware the camera was already past him and the shot was over, or his proximity to the wheels.

Tom Harper, stunt coordinator/second unit director, and I yelled stop, but it was too late. He rolled right into the wheels of the train and as soon as he hit, went limp. He continued to roll lifelessly. I jumped off the gator vehicle and ran to him.

He was unconscious and bleeding from a gash at the top of his head. His thumb was broken, and bleeding, he had some serious injuries.

The Medevac helicopter arrived as he was starting to come around, he had no idea what had happened. He kept asking the same questions over and over, "What Happened, What Happened". He really took a blow to the head. We went to the hospital to see how he was doing, and found him standing outside the emergency room in a hospital gown. He says "get me out of here" I don't like this place. His head wound had been stapled up, his thumb stitched and set. It was time for some rest, and to thank his lucky stars.

Ryan James Happy "The Lone Ranger"

The Charro Saddle
By: Billy Brown

The movie "The Three Amigos", we were in full Charro wardrobe. This scene is kind of funny, but really very lucky for me, I've had all these years to think about it. On this day we were attacking the village - sitting on a hill looking down at the village, about a quarter mile or so. I remember asking someone "What order do we have to be in?" Someone yelled "try and beat me", and then "Just hold up and hit the mark." The mark was at the entrance of the village, Santa Poco.

We heard "Action!" My father as a boy told me "Don't ever run your horse downhill," but here I am with grown up men, doing what dad said not to do, and it was fun and exciting. I was still getting used to my horse. Everyone knew dad and the reason I got the chance to work was because of him. I was grateful for the opportunity. I was in the movies with some great guys.

I thought I had a good Charro saddle, but would soon find out that wasn't the case. I was happy when whoever said "try and beat me", meant I could go all out, and I knew my little horse could run and how he did! I let him go. I hit a spot where I had to check and pick up his head - we were going a little too fast! I pressed hard on my stirrups and picked his head up, and I heard an almost sharp shotgun sound going off under me.

All I remember is looking down, seeing my saddle horn split down the middle. If you know Charro saddles, they are separated in the middle of the seat. The pressure from me pushing down on my stirrups split my saddle down the middle. People behind me saw this broken saddle come flying through the air at them! My horse just kicked it out from behind him. Thank God I didn't fall off!

Mexicans leave the halter and lead rope on when they bridle a horse. They tie the lead rope to their saddle. First lesson I learned in stunts, look for things that can hang you up. I took my fancy lead rope and halter off, so when the saddle split I wasn't tied to my saddle. This marked me a trouble-maker because the Props Department saw me do it and didn't want you messing with their equipment.

They told the head wrangler, Corky Randall, but he saw the reason and let it go. When it was all over, seeing what happened, I was vindicated, if I had tied the rope to my horse and saddle, who knows what could have happened. The Prop guy said he was sorry, and I made a friend.

A Fools, Fool
By: Danny O'Haco

I was cast as a bank robber in the western TV series "The Young Riders." I was also shooting a video for a friend of mine at the same time. We were down south of Tucson on location. I worked it out with my friend to shoot his video the day before I had to be on The Young Riders.

We left our location where we shot the video and headed to the other location. We were running a little late, when I got to base camp everyone was already on set. I rushed and dressed in the wardrobe, and then to the property truck to pick up my gun. I had my scene that day doing dialogue on camera. I can still remember the lines, "You know what I'm going do with my share of the money, I going buy me some cattle and put the rest in the bank."

I ran to the property truck, there is a man in the trailer doing some work. I asked him if I could get a gun. He looks at me and makes a judgement. No sir, I gave out the guns earlier. I chose not to make a scene and argue with him, I knew what would happen later on.

I walked to the set and sat in my cast chair, started going over my lines preparing for my close up later that day. No one even noticed that I wasn't wearing my gun belt and six shooter. After a couple of hours the 2nd Assistant Director, says Mr. O'Haco you are wanted on the set. I walk to the camera and stand on my mark, waiting for direction.   The Director says, "Where is your gun?"

My response was, the Prop man wouldn't give me one. There was silence on the set. Then he repeats what I just said. "The Prop Man Wouldn't Give You One"? It wasn't thirty seconds later I was being strapped with my holster and six gun, they even tied my leg strap for me. I finally got what I was looking for all day, respect.

Bad Case of Cracked Ribs
By: Danny O'Haco

I received a call on my service, Teddy's Answering Service, to call Charlie Croughwell. Charlie was coordinating the stunts for this independent film starring Brad Johnson. He wanted me to double an actor for one day. The scene was for the actor to get shot while crossing over a creek on a pipe line bridge. The pipe line was three foot wide, no hand rails and was 50 foot above the creek floor.

I was to get shot and fall on the pipe line, a friend will come back to rescue me. He picks me up in a firemen's carry, an over the shoulder move, used by firemen when rescuing victims from a fire. The other stuntman shows me how he will do this, I weigh about 145 lbs. He is about 160 lbs., soaking wet. His job was to carry me to the end of the pipe line at a run, where he is shot and we fly off into the side of the creek. At that location on the pipe line the fall would be about 10 ft. in to the side of the bank.

It was quite unnerving to be carried on someone's shoulders going across that bridge with no safety rails, at a full run. As we leave the pipe our bodies separate some and I can't adjust for the landing, we crash into the bank. My chest against his hip. The left side of my rib cage took the impact. Immediately the air was knocked out of me, and the pain was intense on my left side.

Director calls lunch, ½ hour. I'll need every minute to recuperate. I had my stunt bag in the dressing room with ace bandages, and athletic tape. I thought I had just bruised my rib and if I wrapped myself with ace bandages and tape I could continue shooting the scene after lunch.

At this point no one knows how hurt I am, they just assumed I had the air knocked out of me and now I was fully recovered. The Director wants to cover the scene, from the landing, so all we need to do is fall into frame. I lined up behind the other stunt man and tried to land in a similar position from our first fall. Now this is the time to bite the bullet, because it's going to hurt.

We fall into frame, I land on his hip, ribs exposed, the pain shoots through my body like electric shock, and I almost pass out. Then I hear let's do it one more time from this angle. I really don't know how I managed to get through that day, I guess it was just adrenaline.

I couldn't work for three weeks after that, could barely move around the house. But everything worked out eventually.

Khadafy Skoal
By: Bruce Ford

Bruce introduced Khadafy Skoal to the bareback riding in 1989, at The Cheyenne Frontier Days Rodeo. He was the Director that year for the Bareback Riders. Khadafy Skoal had only been bucked in the Saddle Bronc Riding event, to date. He had a reputation for flipping over in the chute, or crushing men against the back of the chute. Horses that do that will hurt you and have to be tied in so that they won't take advantage of a cowboy getting set to ride.

It would be the first time Khadafy Skoal, was bucked in a bareback rigging. Bruce's decision would allow Khadafy Skoal to work in another event. As luck would have it Bruce draws him and wins 1st place and scored 86 points. He took home the check for $6000.00. Winning Cheyenne for the third time. The footage of the ride is in the movie Colorado Cowboy, The Bruce Ford Story.

This amazing horse would go on to buck for 21 years. Retired in 2004 to the Franzen's Ranch in Wyoming, he won the Bareback Horse of the year in 90, 95 & 96. He was also voted the best bareback horse of the National Finals Rodeo, in 94, 96 & 99.

He won millions of dollars for cowboys, over the span of his career. He was legendary in the sport.

His name at birth was S.S. Salty Dog, by the time he was four his name was changed to Khadafy Skoal. He started out on the race track, but had a reputation for bucking jockeys off. He was a natural for the sport of rodeo. His new owners were the Powder River Rodeo Co.

Bruce commented on the horse's talent, he is one of the top three bucking horses ever in the Bareback Riding. Khadafy Skoal passed away March 1st 2015. He was 31 years old.

Bruce Ford:
Winning "Cheyenne Frontier Day" on Khadafy Skoal Photo By: Jennings

What's that Sound

By: Jay Ventress

I was working on the sound stage, and when things got slow, Kim Burke and I would slide off somewhere out of sight and take out our ropes. A saw horse would work perfect for practicing throwing loops.

This is when we found out just how sensitive the microphones used on the set were. We did not know that the sound engineer was having fits when they called for quiet on the set, and the 1st Assistant Director would call out "Sound." There was this swishing sound, and then a sound like something hitting the floor.

This started an all-out search for that sound. Everyone was looking and listening to see if they could find the source. That's when we had to vanish and hide the ropes. I still to this day don't think they ever resolved the origin of that sound.

Priorities
By: Jay Ventress

I worked the studios for 4 years in the late 70's. Kim Burke and I were ropers first, we worked in the studios to get entry fees. Actually it worked out pretty well as we could make good money and could always say we had another job if we wanted to take off. I was a regular on the show called "Paper Chase," about young law students in college. First day I plop myself down in the middle of some of the principal players, so I was established in the main classroom scenes. This worked well for a long time, I had two or three days each week, got a few "silent bits." Life was grand until they told me on Thursday, that they had to re- shoot scenes on Friday.

I told the Assistant Director that I could not be there because I had a prior commitment on Friday. They were very unhappy, really mad is a better term. Needless to say I never worked that show again.

The other "commitment" was a big Jackpot roping in Fallon Nevada. A man has to have his priorities in order, and roping came first.

Happy Face ☺
By: Jay Ventress

I was working on a commercial for McDonalds.
They have their own studio where all McDonalds
commercial are filmed. Everything in the studio
can be moved, counters, tables, chairs etc. The
hamburgers are real, and they had hundreds. The
commercial was going to air in the eastern part of
the United States. The season would be winter,
and there was fake snow everywhere outside. I
am wearing a Mackinaw and bundled up like it's
30 below. The bad news is it's summer in LA,
must have been a 105 at least, I was not a happy
camper, but we all put our Happy Face on and
faked it for the whole day.

Steel Girder
By: Danny O'Haco

The Movie "Kansas" was filmed in the college town of Laurence Kansas in 1988. I was doubling Andrew McCarthy, and we were shooting nights. This night was going to be the fight on the bridge. There is an old steel girder bridge, about 20 feet or so above the water. The scene was for Matt Dillon and Andrew McCarthy to fight on this bridge and go over the railing into the water and continue fighting on the bank of the creek.

I was never a fan of heights, seem I constantly found myself on the ledge of something or other just to test my resolve. Roger Richman was doubling Matt Dillon, and this was the first time that we had worked together. When you choreograph a fight you do it by the numbers. Meaning (1) I duck, (2) I hit you in the jaw, etc. We rehearsed this fight a few times, and it was always to go to the rail facing each other, that way one person wasn't late going over the rail.

We are dressed in wardrobe with wetsuits under our clothes, the water was dirty and cold. Everyone that went into the water had to get a tetanus shot. We had two water specialist in scuba tanks and goggles just in case there was a problem.

Here it is late in night or about 4:00 am, when

they shoot the stunts. I really believe it's done that way in case something does go wrong, the whole night isn't lost. We get in our positions and rehearse a couple of times, every time by the numbers. When the Director calls action the fight begins, we are trading punches, and working our way to the rail. When we hit the rail we are not face to face the way we rehearsed. I have my back to the rail, so I grab Roger which was never in the rehearsal and tried to pivot to the side, but his weight pushed me back into the rail and he goes over, clean shot to the water. I am momentarily balancing on my back trying to find some way to get over. After a second of teetering I finally fall, but I'm not going to clear the steel girders, that are about six feet below the railing.

I go head first into the steel girder with the brunt of the fall on my collar bone and shoulder. That catapults me into a cartwheel and I head for the water. I surface and try to figure out where I am, it's fairly dark and I don't see Roger. Boom! He pops out of the water like Jaws, and grabs me and is dunking me as if to drown me. I only have one arm that is useful, the other is limp and I can't use it. I desperately had to change the venue, no fighting in the water, or I would drown.

I start a side stroke with one arm and kicking my way to creek bank, I get there just before Roger, I move to my back and improvise with my feet, kicking him in the chest as he tries to engage. The mud is so slick Roger can't keep his feet and the fight looks great. No one watching knew that my arm was useless, and if I got to my feet there would be no action. This went on for what seemed like forever, I was hoping to hear cut, and print, because I knew I didn't have another one in me. I didn't have any fractures from the ex-rays, just soft tissue damage, I would be good in a couple of days. This turned out to be a stroke of luck, it kept me on location for the entirety of the show. A broken bone would have had me packing for LA. I guess you got to take the good with the bad.

Who Framed Roger Rabbit
By: Danny O'Haco

Griffith Park, Los Angeles, California was the location for filming "Who Framed Roger Rabbit" the year was 1988. On the road up to the Observatory there is a tunnel, this is where we shot the scenes. The cartoon car, "Benny" was racing out of the tunnel while being chased by the Wiesel's. Our star Bob Hoskins was playing the part of Eddie Valiant, private investigator. I was stunt doubling Bob in this scene, the car comes out of the tunnel and the evil nemesis Christopher Lloyd as Judge Doom, throws a slippery liquid on the pavement. The" Benny" car goes into a skid and crashes in the ditch. Bob Hoskins's character Eddie Valiant, is thrown from the car and lands on his back, unhurt. My job was to do the actual stunt and be thrown out of the car and land on my back. In the movie everything is a cartoon except the actors, so we shoot the scene and the cartoonist draws the characters around us.

This stunt involved a four wheeler that had been modified so a driver could operate it without being seen. We call that in the business, blind driving. In order for this stunt to work, we come out of the tunnel and go into a 360 degree spin, completely in a circle and then crash into the ditch. This is when I fly out over the front of the car and land on my back some fifteen feet away.

I am sitting on top of the four wheeler holding on to a dummy steering wheel, and supposedly there is a cartoon character "Jessica Rabbit," in the seat next to me. I never saw her until I went to the movie.

We put slippery liquid on the road so it would be easier to spin the car. I am belted in with a lap belt, because there are no doors or rails to brace against when you are moving in a circle at a high rate of speed. Charlie Croughwell is doing the driving, and he is an excellent driver.

It's now early morning, and we have been shooting all night, that's usually when the stunt work begins. Our plan was to shoot the car slide and then cut. Our next set up would be the crash scene of me getting thrown out over the front of the car.

We shoot the scene and the car spins perfectly, just what our Director "Robert Zemeckis" wanted. The next scene would involve Charlie to drive the four wheeler into the ditch, the car would be cabled off, and so when we hit the end of the cable, the car would come to an abrupt stop. I get launched into the air and do a summer salt and land on my back. There is no way to practice for this stunt, you have to feel it and go with it. In order to launch me fifteen feet we are going to have to have some speed. If I fall short, that would mean doing it all over again. I have a back pad and hip pads on just in case I miss the sand pile. Director calls "Action" and here we go, hit the end of the cable the car comes to an abrupt halt and I get launched like Evil Knievel, just enough height to do the summer salt and land flat on my back. Bob Hoskins then comes in, they want to see him land in frame. He had a back ground in martial arts, "Judo" and when he went to land in the frame he did a front flip and landed on his back in the exact position I landed in. I was impressed. It was a pleasure working with Bob on this movie, Bob passed away last year. RIP my friend. I had the pleasure of doubling Bob once again on a movie called "Shattered"in1991.

Kathleen O'Haco and Danny O'Haco on the set.

Stake Out
By: Danny O'Haco

The Michael Man Movie, "Heat" was one of the best movies that I've had the privileged to be a part of. Working with Robert De Niro, Al Pacino, and Val Kilmer, and a host of wonderful actors had to be up there as one of the best.

I played a Detective, doing surveillance at this hotel near LA International Airport, on this scum bag criminal. We knew that Robert De Niro's character "Neil McCauley", wasn't leaving town without paying a visit to this double crosser, "Waingro", played so well by Kevin Gage. Our job on this stake out was to watch Waingro's room and let the others know what he was doing.

We are playing cards and eating pizza, while watching the monitor, observing activity in the hall way. Neil McCauley pulls the fire alarm, and the hotel starts evacuating, everyone is asked to leave their room and go to street level.

My partner thinks he is needed down at the front of the hotel and leaves me there. I am watching the monitor when I spot Neil McCauley walking down the hall to Waingro's room. I radio for back up," it's going down on the 17th floor". I'm out the door with gun drawn, in pursuit of Neil McCauley.

Neil McCauley has managed to act like a security guard with a coat and flashlight stolen from the hotels laundry room. He knocks on the door, and turns his back to the peep hole. Waingro doesn't want to cooperate so they dialogue some and then he cracks the door, the door hits Waingro in the face and he is knocked backwards while Neil McCauley enters the room gun pointed at his head.

He shoots this guy in the forehead and is backing out of the room, when I enter behind him with my gun pointed at the back of his head. My lines were "LAPD put your hands on your head now"! McCauley is momentarily surprised, he casually steps back into my gun barrel, and pivots around with his flashlight catching me and my gun. As I start to fall to the floor, he finishes me with a smack to the back of the head with his two foot long flashlight. I am out cold, he moves down to the parking lot, where he ditches Amy Brenneman, then to the airport where he will face off with Al Pacino in the final gun battle of the movie.

The behind the scenes part to this story, was we had to shoot this scene a half a dozen times and each time it got a little more violent. Michael Mann was looking for perfection and he wasn't going to stop until he got what he wanted.

The flashlight was made of hard rubber, but it had some weight to it. Every time Robert De Niro hit me he would ask me if I was all right. I would shrug it off and say, "Don't worry about it"! Next day I had lumps and bruises all over my head, neck, and shoulder. Little mementos from Robert.

Return to Lonesome Dove
By: Jeff Ohaco

I was cast as Carlos the Head Vaquero, on the mini- series," Return to Lonesome Dove". My job as trail boss, was to get this herd of horses from Texas to Montana. Jon Voight's character, Caption Woodrow Call, was determined to drive this herd of wild horses, to his ranch in Montana, and start a breeding operation.

When Captain Call was looking for vaqueros to help him with this horse drive he met up with Nia Peeples who played the part of Agostina Vega. Agostina convinced Captain Call that these horsemen were the best in the world. He needed some convincing, so she takes him to her ranch. Jeff Ohaco, plays "Carlos" her trainer and horse whisperer. Carlos is in the corral and training on a young horse when they walk up and watch. He is reining the horse in a figure eight pattern. This teaches the horse how to change leads and respond to leg pressure, while reining the horse to the left and to the right.

Captain Call calls Carlos over and wants to talk, he wants a little demonstration of Carlos's ability to ride. He takes a scarf off of Agostina and tells Carlos to lay it down in the middle of the corral, then return back to him. Carlos does what he asks, and returns for the next order. Captain Call says pick the scarf up on a dead run and bring it back to me. Carlos doesn't hesitate for a second and sets out at full speed and swoops down off the side of the horse and grabs the scarf, and returns it to Agostina.

From the viewer's point of view, there must have been some trick photography in the execution of that move. Danny asked me, how did you do that? I told him that R.L. Tolbert the stunt coordinator said make it happen Jeff. I had never rehearsed the move before, and my horse had no idea what I was going to do. I had done a similar stunt in Israel while doubling Sylvester Stallone in Rambo III. I picked a goat off the ground when competing in an Afghanistan Sporting event. This was going to be more difficult, the scarf laid flat on the ground.

I remember doing some visualization as how I would do it without falling out of the saddle at a 90 degree angle. I had nothing to hold me, it would have to be all leg strength. First take, and I'm off and running, slide over and time it just right, speed would allow me to create some momentum to return to the saddle.

Down to the ground with my right hand feeling the dirt, and snatching the scarf up in one swoop. A clean run, and I don't know if I could do it again!

Jeff Ohaco and Danny O'Haco
"Return to Lonesome Dove"

The Day Mickey Gilbert Saved My Life,"The Fall Guy" By: Justin Derosa

While on location filming a 2nd unit at Indian Dunes back country, we were doing a driving sequence among some hilly terrain.

Mickey set up a shot that an open "Jeep" was to turn- over, the pipe ramp was set up and cameras were set. The stunt-driver had maybe thirty feet to the ramp, the stunt-driver was going to a grab strap located on the passenger seat, as the Jeep turns over.

Tim Gilbert was up the hill with a radio to send him on his way once Mickey called action, down below the ramp, (note) the pipe ramp had no kicker: Mickey set up various cameras for the roll.

Once everyone was in place and Tim radioed Mickey that he was ready, Mickey, myself, and Gary McLarty dropped back away from the, A, camera. Mickey called action and the stunt-driver came on towards the pipe ramp at about thirty M. P. H.

The Jeep connected with the ramp and slid to the center and launched into a runaway jump, everything happened so fast! Next thing we see is a grill and headlight ten feet away and showing no-sign of slowing.

The driver was holding on to the grab strap laying down under and below the Jeep's dashboard. He thought the jeep was rolling and did not realize what was happening.

Mickey was holding a small video camera, he was filming for the stunt-driver and looking through the view-finder. This all went down in less than twenty seconds. (The Jeep was on us like a Demon from Hell) Mickey grabbed me and pushed me to the right of the jeep, but the jeep still got a piece of my left shoulder and ribs. I went down. As I turned and looked I watched the Jeep hit Mickey Gilbert dead on and run him over, the under carriage ripping and peeling his wardrobe and skin to shreds! After the Jeep hit me and Mickey, it continued on and missed Gary McLarty by inches.

The Jeep did come to a stop and the stunt-driver had no idea what just took place, and yes there were other injuries. That could be another new story in its self.

I started yelling for help as Gary and myself got to Mickey, I remember very clearly me holding Mickey's head and noticed he was knocked out cold. Gary grabbed Mickey and was giving him mouth to mouth and talking into his ear "Don't Go Mickey!" Tim came running down the hill to his Dad, and the look in his eyes said it all. (Unconditional Love for his Father).

Someone called 911 and the skies above our location were filled with News Helicopters. Because of our rugged location no rescue personal could reach us by road. Then out of the blue "Air Rescue Helicopters and Paramedics arrived and air-lifted Mickey out." Mickey survived with no serious injuries, but had many abrasions and contusions. I need to add this to my story, this may help young coordinators and stuntmen and women from preventing an accident like the one on "The Fall Guy". Believe me that wasn't a pretty sight!

The reason the Jeep didn't turn over, and jumped into the air was because the pipe ramp had no kicker at the top. I have designed pipe ramps since the seventies and my pipe ramps have turned over hundreds of vehicles with stunt drivers and never have any gone into a jump. The reason is you (Must) have a kicker, is that it (Guarantee's) it will roll the stunt vehicle, the weight of the engine is what the kicker is for. The kicker snaps the engine over and the body follows. Gravity will bring the vehicle over on its side, and momentum rolls the vehicle over.

I still to this day, design and build Pipe Ramps for major and independent studios, I also assist on sets when requested.

"Kansas" Wally Crowder hitting the pipe ramp

"Kansas"

Danny O'Haco jumping clear

Sell Out
By: Jeff Ohaco

"Hunters Moon" A TV pilot, filmed in Tucson, AZ in 1979. I was called to work extra, as a rider. I was excited to work in the movies, it was my third movie that I had worked on. I was green as grass. Henry Wills was the coordinator, he was retired by this time, and somehow they must have coaxed him out of retirement to do this pilot.

They needed a double for Cliff De Young, one of the leads on the show. I fit the description and someone had told Henry about me, so he called me over to take a look at me. He sized me up and gave me the nod, and was sent to wardrobe. Jeff Ramsey was doubling the other actor, Jeff was living in Tucson at the time and I knew him. I asked him how we should do the saddle fall, to make it look real. He said you have to sell out. Up to this point I thought sell out was a negative term. He explained when I asked "What do you mean Sell Out," you have to go for it as hard and realistically as you can, with everything you got.

The stunt was for us to get shot off our horses, we would not be moving, just standing in place when the twenty bad guys come over the hill and blast us. Seemed like a fairly easy stunt. I remember thinking, I'm working on my SAG card, making the big money, doubling an actor!

Henry told us that when we are shot and on the ground, not to move a muscle, we were supposed to be dead. I was a little nervous because our horses were so close together, there wasn't any room for me to fall, except over the right front shoulder. I told Jeff that's where I was going to fall, he was going off the right side as well. We had our plan, and now was the time for action.

On Action the guns were blazing, I shot out over the shoulder and was laying on the ground next to my horse, with my eyes closed not moving a muscle. I could feel the horses moving around, right next to me. I heard Jeff grunt and groan then silence. The director called cut, and print.

I jumped up and looked over at Jeff, he was pale as a ghost, shaky and holding his arm. It was already starting to swell up, cut and badly bruised was his bicep and it was turning a grotesque color. The horse he fell off of spooked at the gun fire and stepped on his arm and never moved off of it until the director called cut.

Ramsey never moved a muscle during the whole scene, I was in awe, how he did not move even when the horse is standing on his arm. I learned so much that day and it helped shape the way I approached stunts for the rest of my career, Jeff Ramsey "Sold Out" that day, and now I really know what that means.

Rodeo Cologne
By: Danny O'Haco

The German Production Company came to Scottsdale for the Wild West scenery. The commercial was for Rodeo Cologne, and was to be cowboys riding bucking horses in a ranch corral. The Four Peaks area North of Scottsdale was the perfect location for this shoot. Five cowboys including myself were cast to ride bucking broncs for three days.

The old cowboy system of snubbing the bronc to another horse, would be the method of mounting up. This corral at the Four Peaks location, was very rustic, the ground was solid granite, and the corral boards were brittle and weathered. Things were about to get real western.

I choose to be the first rider, we saddled the bucking bronc with a ranch saddle and then I climbed on from the snubbing horse. Once into the saddle I would have to pull a flank strap that was behind me. That would make the horse start bucking. This big sorrel gelding went wild, he seemed to be jumping higher than the fence corral. The still photographers were placed in various spots around the corral to ensure coverage of the action. There were also cameras rolling to capture the scene for the Television audience in Germany.

This went on all day, trading horses and cowboys, after one bucked they would bring in another horse, and a new cowboy would repeat the action. After the second day the cowboys were getting injured and the count was down to four still able to participate. Broken arms, concussions, dislocated fingers, were just some of the injuries sustained. They wanted us to get on four or five a day, and with the conditions of the ground it was becoming a game of attrition for the cowboys. The Producer from Scottsdale said we needed to hire another cowboy, we still had another day to shoot. I was bucked off and knocked unconscious the second day and decided it was time for me to stop.

I had a friend in Mesa that was a former rodeo bronc rider. We recruited him for the final day of filming. After three days and fourteen broncs rides each, we finally called it quits. I believe we were under paid for the danger we were in during the entire shoot. Out of the six who were hired only two made it through without a serious injury.

I never saw the commercial but I can guarantee the German people were in awe when they witnessed the action, and the scenery. It was truly a beautiful place to film and take photos.

The cast of characters were Jeff Ohaco, Jim Scheurn, Steve Geray, John Clemente, myself.

Danny O'Haco "Eve of Destruction"

Jump from Limousine
By: Joyce McNeal-Tolkan

"Cover Up" was a TV series in the 1980's. I was the stunt double for the lead actress, Jennifer O'Neill. Mic Rodgers was the stunt coordinator and double for Jon- Erick Hexum.

My stunt, doubling Jennifer was jumping from a limousine going 25- 30 mph. In the scene I am trying to escape my captors by jumping out the back door of the limo. The vehicle is in motion I open the back door, throw out a brief case and then leap out going down a 45 degree embankment, hitting my mark.

There were five or six other stuntmen on the set that day. My stunt was going to be the last shot of the day. Some of the guys there gave me suggestions on how they would do the jump. The difficulty was the angle of the embankment. I had already decided what would work best for me.

On this particular day, a new young cocky producer came on the set, whom I had never met. He approached me and said, "If you can't do this stunt, I will get in the wardrobe and do it myself." I had been doubling Jennifer on "Cover Up" for a few months and the production was happy with my work. I just looked at him and walked away.

When it was time for my scene, it was already getting late. We had time for one rehearsal and that was it, we had to go. The producer was standing next to Mic when they yelled, "Action" once the car was up to speed, I opened the door, threw out the briefcase and jumped out, with a little help from my friend David Burton. Leaving a good distance of air between my take off, and where I hit the ground and continued rolling down the embankment.

When the producer saw the stunt, he yelled "Oh Shit!" The producer was very happy with the shot, along with the rest of the crew, including Mic.

Joyce McNeal-Tolkan

Roy "Snuffy" Harrison
By: Spice Williams-Crosby

So, I get a phone call from Uncle Gene, aka Judo Gene LeBell, who has mentored my stunt career since 1979. He said in his gruffy voice, "get your ass out here to meet Snuffy. I'm working for him and he wants to meet you!" Apparently, he hired a girl to do a job and she couldn't do it, so he had to let her go. So, of course, when Uncle speaks, a stunt performer would be crazy not to follow through. I met Snuffy and he was gracious, sweet, and very funny! He didn't hire me but promised he'd find something for me.

The girl he let go reported him to SAG for sexual harassment because she was ticked off that he fired her. Everything was proved false and Snuffy was cleared, but it really scared him and a lot of other Stunt Coordinators to think some crazy girl could make up such a horrible story because she got fired for not being able to do her job!

Well, so time went by when I finally got a call from Snuffy to double Katharine Ross on The Colbys TV show. Now, she's so much shorter than me, but apparently we had very similar faces and I was to be drowning and riding in the car. So, height didn't really matter and it was Snuffy's way of truly trying to follow through on his promise. Danny Weselis was doubling some actor on the show and as I was drowning in the ocean, Danny had to dive in, off the pier to rescue me. We laughed all day and had a great time with Snuffy. Next stunt was me sitting in a car as Danny was driving all through these winding roads up in the mountains. Snuffy was doing 2nd Unit with a crew alongside the road as we passed by and a helicopter over head was following us. Needless to say, a simple job but when you bring helicopters you know they've spent some money! That's why Snuffy kept saying to me, "Spice, whatever you do, don't look into the camera as you guys drive by our camera. This is a very expensive day and we have to get everything right and done!" Well, I knew I could follow that order, so we started driving when we heard over the walkie, "remember Spice, don't look into the camera off to the left!"

We drove by and all I heard over the walkie was, "Dammit Spice, I told you NOT to look into the camera!" WHAT? I asked Danny, "Did I look into the camera?" Danny said he was paying attention to the road and the helicopter above so he couldn't tell me. So, we U-turned around, set up again with the helicopter above us and went on "ACTION!" Once again, I heard over the walkie, "Now remember Spice, don't look into the camera!"

When we drove by, I cranked my head so far to the right looking at the mountainside because I did not want to get yelled at again over the walkie and feel like a complete idiot! AGAIN, Snuffy yelled at me, "Dammit Spice, I told you NOT to look into the camera!" At this point I'm begging Danny to watch me because he claims he was paying attention to the road. So, here we go again, turning around, setting up for the helicopter and moving on "ACTION!" Right before we get to the 2nd unit camera with about 7 crew members and Snuffy, I hear Snuffy yelling at me again...."Spice, I told you NOT to look into the camera!" At this point I just thought, "screw it," I cranked my head all the way to the left and yelled back at him, "Snuffy, this is what lookin' into the camera looks like!" Well, there they ALL were, bent over with their pants down to their shoes, flashing their bare behinds at me!!!! Oh, everyone got a great laugh out of it and Danny admitted to being in on it! Ok, Ok, I'm down for a good joke. But, now it was my turn.

We all got back to base camp and were wrapping out when I grabbed Danny and told him that he was now going to be in on my joke. I put a camera in his hands and told him, "Sit on the couch of this honey wagon, tell Snuffy that I'm in the bathroom crying because I felt he had sexually harassed me, and when I come out, you better start takin' photos!!!"

Sure as anything, Snuffy came in lookin' for me to say 'goodbye' and asked where I was. Danny, like he was told to do, told Snuffy that I freaked out and went into the bathroom and was crying! Snuffy immediately ran to the bathroom door, started knocking on it saying, "Spice, Spice, oh man, I'm so sorry. It was just a joke and we didn't mean any harm....please come out so we can talk!" In my sobbing voice, I said, "Snuffy, I will come out to talk to you but I'm really scared!" I heard Snuffy freakin' out and felt it was time...

As I slammed open the door, I came out with only my little G-string panties on and there I was, naked throwing myself all over Snuffy, wrapping my legs around him and telling him, "Smile, Snuffy for the camera!" Danny just snapped away as Snuffy stiffened up his entire body completely speechless and in absolute fear!

Danny and I never laughed so hard in our lives and Snuffy kept those photos in a special drawer, where NO ONE could find them, especially his wife, for many, many years. Don't know whatever happened to them and I've not seen Snuffy for many years. But boy, was he a wonderful stunt coordinator to work for and a very special man that I had the honor to not only work for, but to be able to call him my friend!

Spice Williams-Crosby

The Comebacks
By: Jay Torrez

I was 26 years old when I got my first stunt doubling job on a feature film. The name of the film was "The Comebacks", and I was doubling actor Jesse Garcia doing football stunts. The stunt coordinator was a big time college and professional football player back in the 70's, so he wasn't taking any pity on me even though most of his guys outweighed me by at least 100 lbs.

"The Comebacks" was a spoof of many classic athletic films, but was mainly focused on hacking at movies like "Varsity Blues" and "Friday Night Lights, which were based on the famous West Texas football culture. Needless to say, West Texas is well known for producing some of the best high school football players in the country and there always seems to be a token Hispanic wide receiver in these films (which is very historically accurate).

I get that job of doubling the Hispanic wide receiver. I'm 5'10 and 165 lbs. Taking passes and getting crushed by former professional and NCAA D1 football players was a job that I gladly accepted even though my experience was limited to 2 years of varsity high school football in Belen, NM. We had 2 weeks of rehearsals, which ended up being not much different than a normal college football practice, only we didn't have to do any extra conditioning, which was nice. The warm ups and plays we practiced were adequate to get all of the guys in shape for the shoot, and to be completely honest, that training played a huge part in how I created my own sprint training program that I currently use to stay in shape.

A couple of weeks had gone by where we did a few smaller stunts and some easy football stuff before I had to take a pretty tough tackle and get "dog piled" by 5 other stunt football players. Keep in mind that this film was a comedy, so ridiculous hits and falls are expected. The gag was, the character whom I was doubling catches the kickoff from the opposing team and immediately is annihilated by them. On "action," I received a kickoff, only to take half a step and be greeted by a 6'5' 250 pounder who was actually airborne (post action) at full speed. We initially made helmet contact, followed by some quick backwards hang time, then me being pile driven into the ground. After that, 5 stunt football players jumped on top of us one by one, from 3 foot boxes which were all out of frame. Out of frame means that they were close but not visible from camera's point of view. We ended up doing the gag several times until the director got what he wanted.

I must say that was the most physically taxing stunt that I had ever done. It was just one of those jobs where you know that you are going to be sore the next day no matter how you try to play it out. I am glad that I did this job because it made me feel that I had the nerve to complete a difficult task even though I was very nervous inside. It was my first real "gag" as a Hollywood Stuntman, I was happy, I could make my body work the way in which it needed to work without freezing up in the midst of the chaos. Thank you for the job Alan "Coach" Graf!

Jay Torrez "The Comebacks"

Ben Folds Five
By: Thomas Taylor Goodman

In the late 80's I was approached by a production company from New York. They were going to shoot a music video and wanted me to look over their story boards and let them know if it would be something I wanted to do. After looking at the story boards, I wanted to do this.

I met with the producer and director along with the effects coordinator at his shop. The effects coordinator was showing me all his wonderful toys he had for the video. He had guns, a wind machine, dirt cannon, all kinds of gadgets that we could use. This was my first meeting with the director and he was not sure of my abilities. He asked me if I could do the stunts that were on the story boards. My answer was how much money did he have in his budget?

When he told me how much money they had for the stunt budget, I laughed. He had four major stunts scheduled, a high fall, through a breakaway window, a bar fight and a stair fall. I suggested he go back to the record label and get more money. He wanted to know how many days of shooting to get these stunts on film. Two days tops was my answer.

I didn't hear from him for a week, then he called and said he had the money, but I needed to do the work in two days. The high fall was scrubbed due to the costs. I assured him that everything else would go as planned. His earlier bid from the Hollywood stuntmen said it would take a week to shoot what he wanted.

The first day we blew up a bank, shot the pants off the sheriff, pillaged the town folks. I set my arm on fire to light their cigars, all in all it was a pretty productive day. Day two was the bar fight, stair fall and I was thrown through a window.

The Screen Actors Guild hadn't yet worked up a pay scale for music videos at the time. I charged them four times what I would have made working on a commercial shoot. This video is on you tube, Ben Folds Five, "Underground."

The Rest of the Story
By: Danny O'Haco

In order to bring you my stories from Behind the Scenes I would have to share with you how I transitioned from the Professional Rodeo Cowboys world into the Movie world. I spent 10 years riding the circuit, traveling over a hundred thousand miles and competing at a hundred rodeos each year.

My specialty event was Bareback Bronc Riding. In this event you ride with a bareback rigging. A rawhide handle on a leather body. The animal is judged on his ability to buck, and the cowboy is judged on his ability to ride. The spur ride is what the judges look for.

Bareback Riding is very stressful on the body, physical conditioning plays a role in staying healthy throughout the year. Each cowboy has his own method of doing that. Sit ups and pushups are the most common exercises for maintaining strength. Stretching is very important, to keep muscles loose. Flexibility will keep you from tearing a muscle.

Some of the injuries most common to a Bareback Rider are with the riding arm, and elbow. The hard rawhide handle can cause trauma to the knuckles and the wrist. Athletic tape is used to support the riding arm. Tape is used to keep the elbow from hyperextending, and to support the tendon from elbow to the wrist. Some cowboys like to wear a foam collar to keep the head and neck secure.

Getting bucked off away from your hand can cause you to get hung up. That is the most dangerous aspect of the event. Once a cowboy is hung up to the handle on the rigging he is helpless to free himself from the horse. The horse can inflict injury to the cowboy in this position. The horse can kick your legs out from under you and stomp on your legs and feet as you drag underneath him.

Each year the rodeo seasons opens up with the winter rodeos starting with the Denver Stock Show and Rodeo. These indoor rodeos are very lucrative for the winners, a cowboy or cowgirl can almost guarantee a spot at the National Finals if he or she has a good winter season. El Paso, Fort Worth, San Antonio, Houston, San Angelo, Amarillo. Tucson, Phoenix, Scottsdale, Yuma, Long Beach. These rodeos are from January to March. If you are lucky enough to be consistent during these winter months you are on your way to having a very successful year.

I was lucky enough to win money at rodeos like Houston, Tucson, Scottsdale, Yuma, Long Beach, Phoenix, during the winter months in my career. I won enough money in 1979 to qualify for the National Finals Rodeo which was held in Oklahoma City that year.

Many cowboys that have rodeo in their back round have moved into the stunt business. You can go back to Yakima Canutt, Ben Johnson, Richard Farnsworth and Casey Tibbs just to name a few. Hollywood loved the rodeo cowboy, he could be counted on when the going got tough. The rodeo cowboy's experience with horses and animals was essential in making the "Western." John Wayne and Howard Hawks hired many rodeo cowboys to work on their movies. Jerry Gatlin, Dean Smith, Terry Leonard, Walter Scott, R.L Tolbert, were regulars on the Western Movies in the 60's, 70', 80's.

I retired from the rodeo circuit in 1983, and moved to Tucson Arizona to see if I could find work in the movies. At the time there were movies being made at the Old Tucson Studios. I was cast in an Italian Western movie starring Ethan Wayne, and Ernest Borgnine,   I was cast in a movie "American Justice" starring Gerald McRaney and Jameson Parker. I got a part riding broncs in "Webster" starring Emanuel Lewis with a special guest star Jack Elem. My intention was to get some experience in Tucson and then make my way to Hollywood.

In 1986 an opportunity showed itself, "The Three Amigos" was coming to Tucson to film. I was called in to be a bandito, not a Union contract. Filming was going to start in a couple of days, and the man that Jerry Gatlin had hired to double Tony Plana, "Jeffe " was stuck in Hawaii on Kevin Costner movie "Waterworld" that was over budget. I fit the description that was needed to double "Jeffe," I was only supposed to fill in until Tom could get back over from Hawaii. As luck would have it I was such a good double for Tony Plana, Tom never did take my job away.

When the filming had finished in Tucson, the company moved to Semi Valley CA. Where the set of Santa Poco was built. I made the move with the company and I was now in Los Angeles for good. My career was taking off, and I was fulfilling my dream to work in the movie business. Jerry Gatlin was a former rodeo cowboy, and he was the stunt coordinator. That rodeo connection was at work again, otherwise I would have been playing a bandito for $50.00 a day.

I have to thank many former rodeo cowboys for employing me over the years, on western and non-western productions. One of the best jobs I ever had was doubling Bob Hoskins in the movie "Who Framed Roger Rabbit." My brother Jeff put my name in to double Bob, he was called in by the stunt coordinator, Max Klevin who was good friends with Walter Scott, another rodeo cowboy who was a stuntman and coordinator. Jeff was too tall to double Bob, so he suggested to Max that I would be perfect for the job. They called me in that morning and I got the job doubling Bob Hoskins. I guess being at the right place at the right time could apply as well.

The movie I was hired on in Tucson "American Justice" the stunt coordinator was Bill Burton a former rodeo cowboy. The rodeo connection was at work there as well, also "Webster" which was run by R. L. Tolbert a former rodeo cowboy. My rodeo connections were my life line, and I will always be grateful for that. Hollywood works on connections, the old adage that it's not what you know it's who you know. I would be remiss if I didn't thank my brother Jeff and sister Kathleen and friend Joe Massengale for opening doors.

The Hang Up
By: Danny O'Haco

Rodeo was always full of surprises, one that I recall was in Casper Wyoming. I was riding my bronc when something went wrong. I was bucked off away from my hand, and knew that I was hung up. The horse continues to buck with me along side of him. I am trying to keep on my feet. He is kicking at me and I am taking a beating on my right leg and ankle. This had to be the most vulnerable position I had ever been in.

The pickup men are at a loss on how to help me get free. We go down the area, and I know I have to do something or else I am going to get hurt real bad. The horse has stopped bucking and is just running looking for the corral, while I am dragging on the side. He turns and heads across the arena toward the grand stands, it's a packed Saturday night and the crowd is screaming with horror. They knew that this cowboy was in a pickle.

The horse is heading right for the fence, and I realize that he is going to have to turn one way or the other. If he turns to the left that would give me a second to react. My plan was to do a pony express mount when he stutter steps off the fence. Luck was with me that night, in that split second when he turned to the left I vaulted up on his back and pulled my hand out of the rigging, ejected myself off the right side and landed on my feet. The crowd went wild, they were standing and clapping for my safety. I was saying a prayer that I survived.

My pants and my chaps were torn to shreds, I could feel my ankle and foot starting to swell from the stomping I took. I limped back to the chutes, sat down and started reflecting on how lucky I was to get out of that jam. I got the boot off before the swelling would make it impossible to remove. Slipped into my tennis shoes. I didn't need to see a doctor, only needed some ice.

Every cowboy that rides rough stock will face being hung up. It's not if it will happen, it's when. I had a rough couple of days after that, the next day I was at the western store looking for some new wranglers when the clerk asked me if I was in the rodeo. She then went on to say she attended the rodeo last night and saw the most amazing thing happen. She said she saw this cowboy get drug and kicked around by this horse and then he jumps back on and frees his hand and jumps off right in front of the grand stands. She claimed she never saw anything like that in her whole life. I said yes I saw that, and that guy was me. She couldn't believe I wasn't in the hospital with a cast on my leg. I think that night was when I said to myself, if you can do that on a bucking horse you might have a shot at doing stunt work in Hollywood. There was definitely an overlap between the two careers.

Danny O'Haco on Necklace, Prescott AZ.

"Webster" Emanuel Lewis and Danny O'Haco

"Webster" Jack Elem and Danny O'Haco